Yolanda

PURNELL POCKET GUIDES

The Birds of South Africa

A GUIDE TO 142 SPECIES

Hazel Stokes

Purnell

Cape Town Johannesburg London

Published by
PURNELL & SONS (S.A.) (PTY) LTD.
97 KEEROM STREET, CAPE TOWN, RSA

© *Hazel Stokes* 1979

ISBN 0 360 00446 6

Reproduction
UNIFOTO, CAPE TOWN

Printing and binding
CREDA PRESS, CAPE TOWN

INTRODUCTION

The Purnell Pocket Guide to the Birds of South Africa, which is the first title in a series of South African-related subjects, has been compiled as a compact and easy reference to the birds of South Africa.

From the approximately 800 recorded species the publishers have selected 142 of the most commonly seen birds. These have been arranged to appear in the sequential order adopted in Roberts *Birds of South Africa*.

In most instances the illustrations depict birds in flight in order to emphasise the characteristics not normally evident when a bird is seen standing or perched. A detailed description giving size, distribution and habits accompanies each illustration.

This Pocket Guide has been designed for practical use in the field by amateur ornithologists and nature enthusiasts.

Parts of a bird

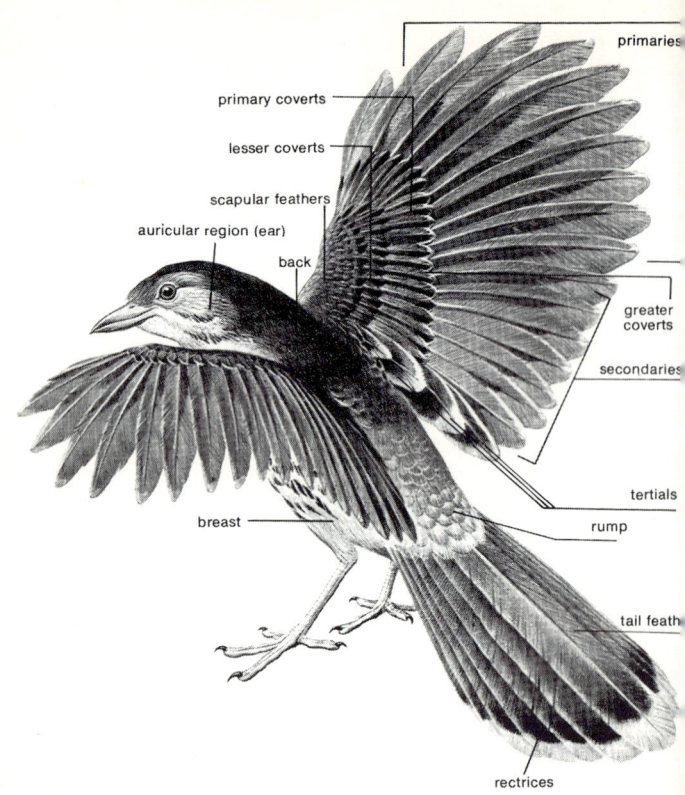

primaries

primary coverts

lesser coverts

scapular feathers

auricular region (ear)

back

greater coverts

secondaries

tertials

breast

rump

tail feath

rectrices

Feet types illustrated show
adaptation in various types of birds

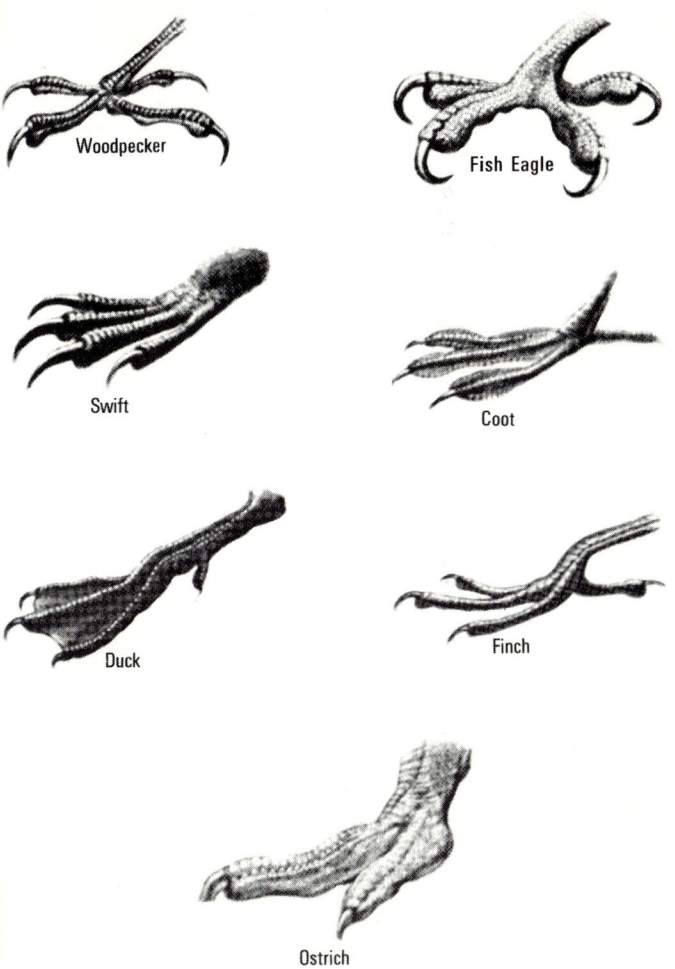

Woodpecker

Fish Eagle

Swift

Coot

Duck

Finch

Ostrich

JACKASS PENGUIN *Spheniscus demersus*
Length: 60 cm. Colour: Black with white waistcoat.
Features: Waddles as he walks. Flippers.
Distribution: Mainly in Cape but also seen throughout coast
of Southern Africa. Eggs: Usually two. Chalky white.

This penguin has been named for its donkey-like braying.
Usually seen in large numbers quietly diving and catching
food under water or just swimming low in water. Has way
of peering inquisitively while it waddles over rocks. Nests in
large colonies making shallow holes.

CAPE PIGEON *Daption capensis*
Length: 40 cm. Colour: Mottled black and white plumage.
Features: Black head. White flashes on tops of wings.
Distribution: Throughout coasts Southern Africa—mainly
out at sea.
Eggs: Does not breed in Southern Africa.

Easy to identify by its mottled plumage. One of the most
common seabirds of our coast. Can be seen picking up food
from the waves, flapping its wings before sailing along.
Usually found in numbers around ships.

CAPE HEN *Procellaria aequinoctialis*
L.: 51-58 cm. Colour: Black all over except white bill and
chin.
Features: Strong, wide wings, bulky body.
Distribution: Throughout coast Southern Africa.
Eggs: Does not breed in Southern Africa.

The most common and largest of petrels that come to these
shores and seen over our seas. A scavenger, it is often seen
sailing on its strong wings near and around fishing vessels,
where it picks up refuse and plankton in the wakes.

JACKASS PENGUIN

CAPE PIGEON

CAPE HEN

STORMY PETREL *Hydrobates pelagicus*

Length: 16cm. Colour: Black and white on rump and wings. Features: Black feet not extending beyond square tail in flight. Distribution: All coastal areas.
Eggs: Does not breed in Southern Africa.

This quiet, dainty, oceanic bird is often seen flying out at sea, or hovering over wake of ship in search of titbits. Appears to be delicately treading the water. Travels the seas of the world.

SHEARWATER (SOOTY) *Procellaria grisea*

Length: 45 cm. Colour: Very dark brown with grey chin and underwings. Features: Delicate build. Long wings.
Distribution: All coastal areas.
Eggs: Does not breed in Southern Africa.

Travels a great distance but is one of the most common of the petrel family seen over the oceans of Southern Africa, especially during the winter months. With its slender streamlined body and long, thin, pointed wings, it may be seen skimming low over the sea, or swooping along the troughs of enormous waves, twisting and rising.

PELICAN (WHITE) *Pelecanus onocrotalus*

Length: 150cm. Colour: White with black-tipped wings. Features: Heavy yellow bill.
Distribution: Throughout Southern Africa but mainly in coastal areas.
Eggs: Two to four. Chalky white.
This stout bird is easily recognized and, in spite of bulk, its flight is a delight to watch. Seen in numbers taking off from the water with dignified ease and flying high on powerful wings. At sunset or sunrise is engaged in fishing until its pouch is full. Makes a nest on the ground of sticks and weeds.

STORMY PETREL

SHEARWATER

PELICAN

GANNET (CAPE) *Morus capensis*

Length: 90 cm. Colour: White with black flight feathers and tip of tail. Features: Distinct black markings round eyes and yellow on head. Gliding flight.

Distribution: Throughout coast of Southern Africa.

Eggs: One large. Chalky white.

This big bird can often be seen flying over the sea following a shoal of small fish, or making a streamlined dive from a great height on to a fish which it pursues under water. Breed by their thousands in crowded colonies on the islands around the coasts of Southern Africa, making valuable guano deposits. Makes low mound for nest.

CORMORANT (WHITE-BREASTED) *Phalacrocorax carbo*

Length: 90 cm. Colour: Black, shiny with white breast.

Features: Four webbed toes. Long neck. Long bill, hooked at tip.

Distribution: All coastal areas and inland waters.

Eggs: Pale blue. Three to five.

Also called Duiker, this bird is often spotted on rock or tree stump with its long wings outspread to dry, or flying in a row with long neck outstretched. Makes a large nest with sticks and weed. Frequently builds up on an old nest.

HERON (BLACK-HEADED) *Ardea melanocephala*

Length: 96 cm. Colour: Black head and neck. Grey underparts. Features: Black-tipped wings. Long neck and bill.

Distribution: Southern Africa. Seen more in the south.

Eggs: Two to four. Pale blue.

One or two are likely to be spotted flying with their necks drawn down within the shoulders, and long legs trailing behind. Often seen standing quietly in a pool or shallow water, with neck slightly stretched up, looking for frogs or fish. Makes a nest of sticks, usually in a small colony or in a lofty tree.

3

GANNET

CORMORANT

HERON

CATTLE EGRET (TICK BIRD) *Ardeola ibis*

Length: 54 cm. Colour: White.
Features: Yellow bill and legs.
Distribution: Throughout Southern Africa, scarce in dry western areas. Eggs: Three to four. Pale greenish blue.

This bird of the heron family is usually seen in flocks in the company of cattle or large game. It differs from other egrets by having a shorter bill and legs. Has yellowish plumes on its head, back and breast in breeding times. Likes to follow the farmer's plough, making a harsh, croaking noise. Nest in heronies, situated near reedbeds.

WHITE STORK *Ciconia ciconia*

Length: 117 cm. Colour: White. Black flight feathers.
Features: Long red bill and legs. Long strong wings.
Distribution: Throughout Southern Africa.
Eggs: Three to five. White.

Seen in large numbers all over, the High Veld especially. A striking bird in flight, flying high with its neck outstretched and legs trailing behind. Is renowned for devouring large number of locusts during its stay. Can be seen roosting in a colony in trees. Some build a nest of large sticks in a tree or on the roof of a building.

CATTLE EGRET

WHITE STORK

HAMMERHEAD (HAMERKOP) *Scopus umbretta*

Length: 50cm. Colour: Rich brown.

Features: Hammer-like head, large wings.

Distribution: Throughout Southern Africa where there is water. Eggs: Three to six. White.

This bird can be seen in streams and ponds shuffling its feet to disturb food. Very distinctive in flight with its rich brown plumage, large wings and hammer-like head. Builds an enormous nest with piles of sticks.

SPURWING GOOSE *Plectropterus gambensis*

Length: 102cm. Colour: Iridescent bronze-green wings and tail. White below and on shoulders. Pink face.

Features: Spur on wing shoulders.

Distribution: Throughout Southern Africa, rarely in the western areas.

Eggs: Six to twelve. Shining ivory.

The largest goose in Southern Africa, the formidable spur on its wing can inflict ugly wounds. Its flight is easy and performed by slow flappings of its wings. Sometimes seen perching or roosting in trees. Makes a well-formed cup for a nest in the reeds.

FLAMINGO (GREATER) *Phoenicopterus ruber*

Length: 140cm. Colour: Pinkish-white body, crimson wings tipped with black.

Features: Long neck, heavy curved bill, long legs.

Distribution: Throughout Southern Africa.

Eggs: Do not usually breed in Southern Africa.

May be seen flying in formation with their long necks and legs outstretched, and often spotted on the water's edge in large numbers in various attitudes. It sieves through the sludge on the bottom of the water for food with the upper mandible inverted. Its nest is a mound of mud with a hollow top.

HAMMERHEAD

SPURWING GOOSE

FLAMINGO

SACRED IBIS *Threskiornis aethiopicus*

Length: 89 cm. Colour: White with black head and neck, black-tipped wings.
Features: Bare head and neck, long heavy curved bill.
Distribution: Cape and eastern half of Southern Africa.
Eggs: Two to four. Chalky white sparsely marked with reddish brown.

This was the sacred bird of ancient Egypt. Seen on the banks of rivers, lakes and swampy places, standing erect with its heavy curved bill resting on its breast, or flying in formation with its bare black rubbery neck outstretched.
Nests in colonies in trees or reeds.

EGYPTIAN GOOSE *Alopochen aegyptiacus*

Length: 71 cm. Colour: White shoulders and black flight feathers light below. Features: Brown horseshoe shape on chest. Reddish brown ring round eye.
Distribution: Throughout Southern Africa except western areas.
Eggs: Seven to nine. Polished creamy colour.

This handsome goose is seen mostly where there is permanent water and in wheat areas. In small or large parties, sometimes perched in trees where it likes to roost. Nesting sites vary and the geese sometimes take over large nests of other birds.

YELLOW-BILLED DUCK *Anas undulata*

L.: 51-58 cm. Colour: Mottled grey.
Features: Yellow bill, brown legs.
Distribution: Throughout Southern Africa.
Eggs: Six to ten. Yellowish cream.

The most common duck in South Africa, seen usually in large parties sitting high in the water, or flying off in formation. Is gregarious and makes a rounded hollow for a nest.

6

SACRED IBIS

EGYPTIAN GOOSE

YELLOW-BILLED DUCK

SECRETARY BIRD *Sagittarius serpentarius*

L.: 125-150cm. Colour: Grey with orange round eye. Black legs and tip of tail. Features: Bunch of quill-like feathers from crown. Very long legs.
Distribution: Southern Africa, mainly in dry areas.
Eggs: Two to three. White, sometimes brown-spotted.

An indigenous bird, often seen stalking on its long legs over the veld. May be spotted spreading its wings to protect itself while stamping on a snake, or dealing with it with its eagle-like bill. The nest is a large platform of sticks.

VULTURE (CAPE) *Gyps coprotheres*

L.: 105-115cm. Colour: Blue head and neck. Buff underparts. Wings light brown. Features: Ruff of white feathers round neck. Large wings. Bare head and neck.
Distribution: Throughout Southern Africa.
Eggs: One. White.

This huge bird is commonly seen around mountains, soaring high in the sky, wheeling and gliding on its huge wings. When looking for food, its wonderful eyesight often enables it to discover even a well-concealed carcass. Makes a small cup-shaped nest of grass on a mountain ledge.

LANNER *Falco biarmicus*

L.: 40-45 cm. Colour: Blackish and dark grey above and tail. Chestnut below. Features: Pointed wings, underparts strongly barred. Distribution: Throughout Southern Africa. Eggs: Three to four. Cream closely speckled with reddish-brown.

A falcon, usually seen in pairs mainly in mountainous districts. Can be spotted making a bold spectacular swoop on to its prey from a great height. Nests on a high ledge of a cliff or in a thick bush.

SECRETARY BIRD

ULTURE

LANNER

ROCK KESTREL *Falco tinnunculus*

L.: 30-33 cm. Colour: Bright chestnut back and underparts. Blue-grey head and tail. Rich dark-brown wings. Features: Barred tail. Pointed wings.
Distribution: Throughout Southern Africa.
Eggs. Four. Cream heavily mottled with brown.

This handsome bird can be seen hovering with rapidly beating wings over one place for a prolonged period, or appearing motionless in the sky for a time. Takes over old nests of other birds.

BLACK-SHOULDERED KITE *Elanus caeruleus*

Length: 30 cm. Colour: Grey wings with black shoulders. White below. Features: Black shoulders shown in flight. Pale looking.
Distribution: Throughout Southern Africa.
Eggs: Three to four greenish-white, boldly marked with brown.

One of the smallest and most common of the hawk family. Often seen perched on telegraph poles, or hovering quietly before dropping straight down on to its prey. Prefers open country where there are a few trees. Has a pleasant clear, piping whistle. Uses old nests of other birds.

BLACK EAGLE (VERREAUX'S) *Aquila verreauxi*

Length: 88cm. Colour: Mainly black and white.
Features: Black V band on back.
Distribution: Throughout Southern Africa.
Eggs: One to two. Blotched with brown.

This magnificent eagle can be seen circling round mountain tops, easily identified by the band of white on the centre of back and rump. Builds a bulky nest on a ledge or in a stunted tree.

ROCK KESTREL

BLACK-SHOULDERED KITE

BLACK EAGLE

CROWNED EAGLE *Stephanoaëtus coronatus*

L.: 80-90 cm. Colour: Black above. Light below, mottled and barred. Chestnut on wings. Features: Large crest. Heavily barred long tail. Powerful feet and talons.
Distribution: Throughout Southern Africa except Cape Peninsula. Eggs: Two. White, sometimes with rusty streaks.

A fierce bird of the forest, it preys on small buck and monkeys. May be seen soaring high above the forest on its short rounded wings, or sitting high in a tree, where it builds its large nest, which lasts for many years.

HARRIER EAGLE (BLACK-BREASTED) *Circaetus pectoralis*

L.: 63-68 cm. Colour: Dark brown wings, head and neck. White body, light-grey legs.
Features: Barred tail. Strong flight.
Distribution: Throughout Southern Africa.
Eggs: One. White, sometimes blotched with brown.
In flight the dark breast is clearly defined against the white underparts and light under wings. Often seen soaring up in the sky in open places or dashing off with a snake in its talons. Constructs a platform with a cup lined with soft vegetation.

FISH EAGLE *Haliaëtus vocifer*

L.: 63-73 cm. Colour: White front, back and tail. Black wings. Chestnut belly. Features: Screams as it dives.
Distribution: Throughout coast Southern Africa and inland water expanses.
Eggs. Two. Pure white.

This handsome bird lives mainly on fish. Usually seen in pairs on rocks at low tide, or, in the air, before making a spectacular stoop at a fish. Makes enormous nest high up in large tree which it uses for years.

CROWNED EAGLE

HARRIER EAGLE

FISH EAGLE

BATELEUR EAGLE *Terathopius ecaudatus*

L.: 55-70 cm. Colour: Black body, white wings with black tips. Chestnut black and tail. Red on face and legs. Features: Pointed broad wings, short tail and large head. Distribution: Throughout country except Cape Peninsula. Eggs: One. Creamy-white.

A handsome eagle, characteristic of Southern Africa. It cannot be mistaken with its spectacular flight and richly-coloured wings. Sometimes a loud clapping from its wings can be heard. A smallish, flat nest is made high in a tree.

JACKAL BUZZARD *Buteo rufofuscus*

L.: 44-53 cm. Colour: Black above. Grey under wings. Rufous below. Features: Broad strong wings. Chestnut tail with single black bar.
Distribution: Throughout Southern Africa except dry areas.
Eggs: Two. White smeared with mauvish-brown.

This bold hawk is usually seen soaring around the slopes and tops of hills, or hovering with slow wing beats looking for prey. Its name is derived from its jackal-like cry. Builds a deep cup-like nest with sticks in a high tree or ledge.

STEPPE BUZZARD *Buteo buteo*

L.: 45-50 cm. Colour: Dark brown above, lighter below, streaked with brown. Features: Broad wing and tail.
Distribution: Throughout Southern Africa.
Eggs: Does not breed here.

A common migrant from the north, seen mostly in the open and savanna veld. Spends a lot of time in flight, soaring round at a great height. Can be spotted sitting on a tall fence post or telegraph pole, looking for prey. Has remarkable eyesight.

BATELEUR EAGLE

JACKAL BUZZARD

STEPPE BUZZARD

AFRICAN GOSHAWK _Accipiter tachiro_

L.: 37-39 cm.. Colour: Dark grey-brown above, lighter below. Features: Broad bars on tail. Large wings.
Distribution: Eastwards and north of Southern Africa.
Eggs: Two to four. White.

This handsome hawk may be seen dashing through the thicket at a low height after a small bird. Sometimes can be spotted riding its prey down to the ground from a great height. If seen circling in the sky on strong wings, the narrowly barred underparts can be seen. Makes a nest of twigs in a tree.

CHANTING GOSHAWK _Melierax musicus_

L.: 53-63 cm.. Colour: Blue-grey, white below with grey cross-bars. Features: Long wings. Noted for chanting call.
Distribution: All dry areas of Southern Africa.
Eggs: One to two. Bluish white.
This handsome bird is often seen perched on a tree or telegraph pole quietly looking for prey, or sailing leisurely over the veld. Its chanting call is seldom heard. Makes a flat nest in a thorn tree or bush.

MARSH HARRIER (AFRICAN) _Circus ranivorus_

L.: 44-49 cm. Colour: Dark brown above, nape lighter, broadly streaked with black. Chestnut below. Underside wings light grey.
Features: Long grey barred tail. Long wings and legs.
Distribution: Southern Africa. Eggs: Three to five.

This bird likes swampy and marshy country and can be seen soaring high in the air or beating its wings slowly as it passes low over reedbeds. It includes young birds in its diet of small mammals and eggs. Flattens a place in the reeds or grass for a nest.

AFRICAN GOSHAWK

CHANTING GOSHAWK

MARSH HARRIER

MONTAGU'S HARRIER *Circus pygargus*

L.: 40-47 cm.. Colour: Pearl-grey above, pinkish-red under-parts, streaked with chestnut. Features: Dark bar across very long wings, prominent bars on tail. Black-tipped wings. Distribution: Southern Africa except western Cape. Eggs: Does not breed here.

This migrant from Europe is seen mostly around grassy and scrub countryside. Rather a silent bird, often spotted flying with leisurely flapping wings then pouncing down on a prey with agile banks and turns.

FRANCOLIN (GREYWING PARTRIDGE) *Francolinus africanus*

Length: 33 cm. Colour: Tawny mottled black. White streaks. Features: Flight feathers dusky grey, rises with shrill squeak. Distribution: Confined to the south. Eggs: Four to eight. Ochre speckled and spotted with dark brown.

Occurring mostly on grassy slopes and stony hillsides. It can be easily recognized in flight by its grey-brown rotund body; and short rounded wings. If flushed a covey will fly up and scatter in all directions with shrill squeaks. Puts its eggs under a tuft of grass.

HARLEQUIN QUAIL *Coturnix delegorguei*

Length: 18 cm. Colour: Dark brown above, underpart chestnut. Neck white. Black Bib. Features: White throat, encircled by black. Distribution: Throughout Southern Africa mainly Eastern Cape. Eggs: Five to ten. Cream with large brown blotches and spots.

A pugnacious little game bird, easily identified, can b spotted in large numbers running about in grassland o crops. Makes a rough scrape in the ground under a tuft c grass for a nest.

MONTAGU'S HARRIER

FRANCOLIN

HARLEQUIN
QUAIL

CROWNED GUINEAFOWL *Numida meleagris*

L.: 53-58 cm. Colour: Black and white thickly spotted plumage, blue neck, red on head.
Features: Drooping hindquarters, bony knobbly crown.
Distribution: Widely spread over Southern Africa.
Eggs: Seven upwards to twenty. Buff finely speckled with dark brown.

Parties can often be seen running about in thick grass and thicket or feeding quietly on insects and seeds. Roost in trees at night. Makes a scrape in the ground for nest.

COOT (RED-KNOBBED) *Fulica cristata*

Length: 43 cm. Colour: Sooty black all over.
Features: Two red knobs at base of white bill.
Distribution: Throughout Southern Africa.
Eggs: Four or more. Stone colour finely speckled with dark brown.

Can be spotted on open sheets of water throughout Southern Africa. It can be watched scurrying across the water chasing other water fowl in a bullying manner, or quietly feeding on the banks on water plants and insects. Builds a nest of a heap of weeds in the water among the reeds.

CROWNED CRANE *Balearica regulorum*

Length: 105 cm. Colour: White wings with dark tips. Buf back, grey underneath.
Features: Golden crown and red wattle from chin.
Distribution: Mainly in north and east of Southern Africa
Eggs: Two. Bluish white.

Found mostly in marshy districts or near stretches of water A beautiful, decorative bird much given to dancing and display. Has a joyful, ringing call. It takes its name from its crown—a bunch of soft golden quills. Makes a large nes in reeds.

CROWNED GUINEAFOWL

COOT

CROWNED CRANE

WATTLED CRANE *Bugeranus carunculatus*

Length 120cm. Colour: White neck and chest, grey back and black underparts and wings. Black head, red bill.
Features: Wattles hanging either side of face.
Distribution: Swampy veld over most of Southern Africa except western areas. Eggs: Two. Sandy-coloured dappled.

A stately bird in flight, its white gleaming neck can be spotted at a distance. Can frequently be seen in small parties. Like the Crowned Crane it displays and dances. Makes a grass nest on the ground.

BLUE CRANE *Tetrapteryx paradisea*

L.: 105 cm. Colour: Grey-blue.
Features: Large round head. Long dark plumes over tail.
Distribution: Scattered all over Southern Africa.
Eggs: Two: buffish brown with long streaks and blotches of brown.

This stately crane is the national bird of South Africa. Generally seen in pairs in damp grassy country. Its wing-beat is slow and steady. Often can be spotted foraging with its strong bill in fields of stubble. Sometimes kept as a pet. Makes a scrape in the ground for its nest.

KORI BUSTARD (GOMPOU) *Otis kori*

Length: 135cm. Colour: Brownish-grey upperpart, neck and head mottled in black and white with narrow lines. Brown wings with white below. Features: Long legs and neck. Crested nape. White stripe over eye. Broad wings.
Distribution: Seen throughout Southern Africa.
Eggs: One to two. Olive mottled with dark brown.

The most common and the biggest bustard seen in Southern Africa. Usually spotted as it moves over the veld with long stately strides, or running very fast, or flying with long neck and legs outstretched. Does not bother to build nest. Lays eggs on bare ground.

WATTLED CRANE

BLUE CRANE

KORI BUSTARD

JACANA (AFRICAN) *Actophilornis africanus*

L.: 25-30 cm. Colour: Rich chestnut body and wings. Black on head and neck, with white and golden yellow.

Features: Long tapering toes. Large wings.

Distribution: Southern Africa, mainly in the east.

Eggs: Three to five. Long, buff marked with black lines and streaks.

Also called the Lily-trotter. Usually seen skirting the edge of the water looking for food in the weeds. A graceful bird with curious long toes. It has a way of walking daintily on the floating leaves of aquatic plants. The nest is a meagre collection of weeds on the water's edge.

BLACK OYSTER CATCHER *Haematopus moquini*

Length: 51 cm. Colour: Black.

Features: Long red bill and red legs.

Distribution: West and south coast.

Eggs: One to four. Light stone colour with sepia markings and blotches of pale grey.

Usually seen in pairs, especially where it is sandy. It is interesting to watch it among the rocks, prising open a mollusc shell with its odd wedged beak. Makes a nest among the pebbles.

TURNSTONE *Arenaria interpres*

Length 23 cm. Colour: White underneath with dusky-brown band on chest and dark-brown wings.

Features: Orange legs, upturned bill. Shows patch of white on back and wings in flight.

Distribution: All coastal areas.

Eggs: Does not breed here.

Although this bird breeds in the north, it spends most of its time about Southern Africa. Commonly seen on the rocks and quite often on inland waters. Probes around with its upturned bill in seaweed and rocks looking for crustacea on which it subsists. It has a general tortoiseshell appearance.

JACANA

BLACK OYSTER CATCHER

TURNSTONE

RINGED PLOVER *Charadrius hiaticula*

Length 16 cm. Colour: Brown umber above, forehead black with white band. White below, with broad black band on chest. Orange legs.
Features: White band on wings in flight.
Distribution: Throughout Southern Africa.
Eggs: Does not breed here.

A very common visitor from the north, seen mainly on the coast, but very often inland on large sheets of water. Plump and tawny, this little wader can be seen feeding on the sands, making sudden little runs with halts, while emitting a soft mellow piping.

SANDPLOVER (WHITE-FRONTED) *Charadrius marginatus*

Length 18 cm. Colour: Pale, sandy. Black line behind eye.
Features: Darting run. Down-turned tip to bill.
Distribution: Throughout coast of Southern Africa.
Eggs: Usually two. Deep cream with dark brown spots and streaks.

Indigenous species of Southern Africa seen all year round on sand dunes. Its pale colouring makes it difficult to spot, until it starts running in its amusing way—singly or in small parties. Takes sudden flight after sand flies. Partly covers eggs with sand.

CROWNED LAPWING (PLOVER) *Stephanibyx coronatus*

Length 30 cm. Colour: Pale brown above, white underneath, black tail and wingtips.
Features: Black crown, red bill and legs.
Distribution: Throughout Southern Africa.
Eggs: Two to four. Buff with smudges of sepia.

It is often discovered by its shrill scream when a person approaches its nest. This scream is aptly described by its Afrikaans name 'Kiewietjie'. Generally seen in pairs. Utters a loud whistle at night. A scraped hollow in peaty soil or in short grass serves as a nest.

RINGED PLOVER

SANDPLOVER

CROWNED LAPWING

BLACKSMITH PLOVER *Hoplopterus armatus*

Length: 30 cm. Colour: Black and white.

Features: Underwings and wing coverts grey. White head, and general black and white appearance.

Distribution: Throughout Southern Africa except dry areas in the west.

Eggs: Two to five. Brownish with black blotches.

This bird derives its name from the harsh clinking noise it makes when disturbed, rather like a hammer on an anvil. Spotted on open grassland where cattle feed, usually not far from water. It may be seen lifting its wings aggressively near its nest, a depression in the grass, lined with dry leaves.

AFRICAN SNIPE (ETHIOPIAN) *Capella nigripennis*

Length: 28 cm. Colour: Brown with white lowerparts.

Features: Long bill, black eyestripe.

Distribution: Throughout Southern Africa.

Eggs: Two. Pale olive-green spotted with tones of brown.

This bird is found near marshy ground. At nesting time a strange, drumming sound can be heard. This is caused by vibration of the outer tail feathers as the bird dives to the ground. Makes a nest in tufts of grass.

CURLEW SANDPIPER *Calidris ferruginea*

Length 28cm. Colour: Mottled buff and black, lower neck and rump white.

Features: Long down-curved bill.

Distribution: Throughout Southern Africa, on coast and lakes.

Eggs: Does not breed here.

This wader is a common visitor to Southern Africa. Seen usually in large numbers on sheets of water, probing around for food, rising into a buoyant flight.

BLACKSMITH PLOVER

AFRICAN SNIPE

CURLEW
SANDPIPER

LITTLE STINT *Calidris minuta*

Length: 14cm. Colour: Mouse-brown and white.
Features: Small size, light V mark on back in flight.
Distribution: Throughout Southern Africa.
Eggs: Does not breed here.

This diminutive wader comes from the Arctic where it breeds. Common and abundant, seen on our shores and inland waters, usually in the company of other waders, on mud banks. Makes a tweeting sound when taking off in flight.

SANDERLING *Crocethia alba*

Length: 19 cm. Colour: Greyish-white, black legs and bill.
Features: Pointed bill. White wing stripe conspicuous in flight.
Distribution: Throughout coasts of Southern Africa.
Eggs: Breeds only in Arctic.

Seen on beaches, the little black legs of this bird twinkle rapidly as it chases a breaking wave while it dashes in for food—marine animals which have been washed up. Usually seen in small parties. Tame and amusing to watch.

RUFF *Philomachus pugnax*

Length: 30 cm. Colour: Sepia above. White, pale sepia on chest. Features: Conspicuous dark centres to feathers. Long yellow or orange legs. Longish bill.
Distribution: Throughout Southern Africa.
Eggs: Does not breed here.

One of the largest wader migrants. In the summer months, it can be spotted in company with other waders on the edge of water preening itself, or taking off. Rather a silent bird.

LITTLE STINT

SANDERLING

RUFF

GREENSHANK *Tringa nebularia*

Length 32cm. Colour: Buff brown above streaked light and dark. White below.
Features: Long, greenish legs and long sharp bill.
Distribution: Throughout Southern Africa.
Eggs: Does not breed in Southern Africa.

This large wader is usually seen singly or in small groups. It is a conspicuous elegant bird and easily recognized in flight by the white patch on its rump and tail. Makes a loud resonant call when disturbed.

AVOCET *Recurvirostra avosetta*

Length: 43 cm. Colour: Snowy-white and black.
Features: Slender up-curving bill and long legs.
Distribution: Throughout Southern Africa.
Eggs: Three to five. Pale buff, dark spots and lines with mauve undermarkings.

A common migrant from the north, although sometimes breeds here. A beautiful and conspicuous wader. Seen usually feeding in flocks, in water, using its unique bill in a sideways manner to scoop up some aquatic insect.

GREY PHALAROPE *Phalaropus fulicarius*

Length 18cm. Colour: Grey and white.
Features: White bar on wing and on underparts. Pointed bill.
Distribution: Around the southern coastline.
Eggs: Does not breed here.

A dainty little wader, often seen in small parties off the sea-shore swimming like a coot. Has a habit of going round in circles in search of food. After breeding in the north, it adapts itself remarkably to aquatic life for migrating.

GREENSHANK

AVOCET

GREY PHALAROPE

DIKKOP (CAPE) *Burhinus capensis*
Length: 44cm. Colour: Mottled grey and brown above white with streaks below.
Features: Thick knees, large eyes with white stripe.
Distribution: Throughout Southern Africa.
Eggs: Two. Dull buff with brown smudges.

Usually found near water where it finds its food. During the day, it lies quietly in the scrub but at dusk it moves off with a plaintive cry which often continues through the night. It lays its eggs on bare ground.

DOUBLE-BANDED COURSER *Rhinoptilus africanus*
Length 22cm. Colour: Mottled brown above and light below. Grey legs. Rufous wings.
Features: Two black bands on chest. Piping call.
Distribution: Mainly in western areas of Southern Africa and usually in dry, sandy places.
Eggs: One. Creamy marked with thin brown scrawls.

This little bird is not easily seen as it blends with its surroundings. But it can more easily be spotted when it is running about. Makes a slight scrape in ground for nest.

BLACK-BACKED GULL *Larus dominicanus*
Length: 60 cm. Colour: White with black back and wings. White wing-tip. Features: Long wings. Yellow bill and legs.
Distribution: Throughout coast Southern Africa.
Eggs: Two to three. Olive-brown with large brown splotches.

A very common gull on our coastline and often seen with its splendid wings outspread, gliding around as it looks for food. A pirate and a scavenger, it plunders other birds' nests for eggs and young and likes refuse which it finds in ports. Nests in open in a colony. Scrapes a depression in soil.

DIKKOP

DOUBLE-BANDED COURSER

BLACK-BACKED GULL

GREY-HEADED GULL *Larus cirrocephalus*

Length: 43 cm. Colour: Pale grey body. Dark grey head.
Features: Graceful bird with light-coloured eye. Hooked bill.
Distribution: Most large inland waterways and coastal regions mainly in east.
Eggs: Two to three. Olive green with brown and grey splotches.

A common gull and similar to the smaller Hartlaub's Gull which has a white head. Both are scavengers, living on animal matter and, like most gulls, rob other birds of their young and eggs. Makes nest of a floating heap of weeds.

TERN (COMMON) *Sterna hirundo*

Length: 33 cm. Colour: Light grey with black-tipped wings.
Features: Red bill and legs. Pointed, slender wings and forked tail.
Distribution: Throughout coast Southern Africa.
Eggs: Does not breed in Southern Africa.

Easily distinguished from a gull by its wings and bill, it has a way of suddenly diving from a great height into a wave to catch a fish with its pointed bill. Flocks may be seen making a great commotion attacking a shoal of sardines.

ROCK PIGEON (SPECKLED) *Columba guinea*

Length: 33 cm. Colour: Grey with rich brown on upperparts and wings. Chestnut collar.
Features: Red eye. White speckles.
Distribution: Throughout Southern Africa except for a central section.
Eggs: Two. White glossy.

This large pigeon is a powerful flier and is usually seen in small flocks where there are rocks. Feeds on the ground in open country. Frequently a nuisance to farmers as it eats fruit and grain. Nests in holes of trees and buildings.

GREY-HEADED GULL

TERN

ROCK PIGEON

OLIVE PIGEON (RAMEROON) *Columba arquatrix*

Length: 40 cm. Colour: Dark wine. Grey head.
Features: Spotted white on chest and wings. Yellow bill and feet. Distribution: Southern Africa in well-wooded areas.
Eggs: One. Glossy white.

This conspicuous bird is one of the largest pigeons found in Southern Africa. Often seen in large numbers feeding on fruit in the tops of trees. Makes a heavy flapping noise with its wings when it flies off. The nest is a scanty platform of twigs.

RED-EYED DOVE *Streptopelia semitorquata*

L.: 33-36 cm. Colour: Head, neck, throat to belly dove-grey. Brown umber across back and wings.
Features: Broad black half-collar. Red eye.
Distribution: Southern Africa, except western dry areas.
Eggs: One to two. White.

Quite tame and common, often spotted in well-watered wooded places, making a clatter when a number of them fly off. Its red eye and shorter tail distinguishes it from the Turtle Dove. Builds a nest of twigs not far from the ground.

LAUGHING DOVE *Stigmatopelia senegalensis*

Length 25cm. Colour: Blue-grey above head, neck and chest rich lilac. Mantle tawny.
Features: White on outside of tail, when in flight.
Distribution: Throughout Southern Africa.
Eggs: Two to three glossy white.
Very often seen quietly feeding in large parties on the ground. Has a gentle chuckling call. A similar bird, a bit larger with a black half-collar is called Turtle Dove. Builds a scanty nest low in a tree or bush.

OLIVE PIGEON

RED-EYED DOVE

LAUGHING DOVE

NAMAQUA DOVE *Oena capensis*

Length 27cm. Colour: Black and white, and grey. Upperpart earthy-brown. Features: Long graduated tail. Face, throat to chest black. Distribution: Throughout Southern Africa. Eggs. Two. Pale yellow.

A small pretty little dove, very often seen in parties in open grassy country, feeding on grass seeds. It flies very swiftly and fans out its tail when it alights. Makes a small platform of stems and twigs for a nest.

LOURIE (KNYSNA) *Tauraco corythaix*

Length: 47 cm. Colour: Crimson flight feathers. Green and blue-purple plumage. Features: Rounded crest. Long tail. Distribution: Forest coastal belt to Natal and East Africa. Eggs: Two. White.

A strange, beautiful bird which is peculiar to Southern Africa (a grey species occurs in more open country further north). This richly-coloured bird can be seen as a glowing mass of feathers, flying in a heavy bouncy way, or running about the trees, in small parties. Makes a nest of sticks in a tree.

RED-CHESTED CUCKOO *Cuculus solitarius*

Length: 30 cm. Colour: Dark grey above. Buffish below. Features: Bars on belly. Chestnut chest. Persistent call. Distribution: Throughout Southern Africa, in wooded parts. Eggs: Glossy olive. Usually parasitizes the Robin's nest.

One of the largest and best-known of the many cuckoos in the country. Its Afrikaans name is derived from its three syllable call sounding like piet-my-vrou. Heard persistently throughout the spring and early summer. Usually hidden in foliage it is more often heard than seen. Has a swift flight.

NAMAQUA DOVE

LOURIE

RED-CHESTED CUCKOO

KLAAS'S CUCKOO *Chrysococcyx klaas*

Length 18cm. Colour: Green above. White below.
Features: Broad white patch when tail is expanded. Ringin
call.
Distribution: Throughout Southern Africa.
Eggs: Varied in colour.

This pretty little cuckoo can often be heard, giving a thi
monotonous cry, before it is spotted in its swift flight throug
the trees, sometimes seen in open rocky countryside. Lay
its eggs in other birds' nests.

COUCAL (BURCHELL'S) *Centropus superciliosus*

Length: 38 cm. Colour: Rich chestnut back and wings. Dar
head cream below.
Features: Curved bill and broad, rounded tail.
Distribution: Eastern and southern half of country.
Eggs: Three to five. Round white.

A handsome, skulking bird, does not fly high. Often see
crouching on the bush near a stream or riverbed. Emits
mournful gurgling sound. Makes a nest of a dome-lik
structure in a bush near the ground.

KLAAS'S CUCKOO

COUCAL

BARN OWL *Tyto alba*

L.: 30-33 cm. Colour: Golden buff and grey, mottled blac
and white. Golden underparts, flecked brown. Features
Dusky bars on wings and tail. Pale heart-shaped facial disc
Distribution: Throughout Southern Africa.
Eggs: Two to nine. White.

This cosmopolitan bird has always been closely associate
with man. Sometimes seen floating away from a buildin
or tree at dusk, going to hunt rodents for supper. Whils
roosting in a barn or hollow tree, it can be heard making a
eerie snoring noise. Nests in a hollow tree, roofs of building
or crevice in rocks.

GRASS OWL *Tyto capensis*

L.: 34-37 cm.. Colour: Rich dark brown. Creamy underparts
Features: White facial disc. Head looks as if it has a dark cap
Distribution: Eastern and southern parts of Southern Africa
Eggs: Three to four. White.

This dusky brown owl with a white face, is often spotted i
open grass country, making a short flapping flight low ove
the grass before settling. Makes a curious hissing sound
Hollow in the ground hidden under grass for a nest.

MARSH OWL *Asio capensis*

L.: 36-37 cm.. Colour: Sepia on back and neck, and lighte
below. Features: Pale facial disc. Dark ring round eyes
Slightly barred tail.
Distribution: Throughout Southern Africa except wester
areas.
Eggs: Three to four. White and glossy.

At dusk you can see this almost tame owl flying in a party
It frequents damp places and grassy swamps. Emits a
curious frog-like croak. Nests in a hollow on the ground, i
grass or rushes.

BARN OWL

GRASS OWL

MARSH OWL

SCOPS OWL *Otus scop*

L.: 18-20 cm. Colour: Mottled, grey, buff and brown.
Features: Small. Ear tufts. Leaf-like appearance.
Distribution: Southern Africa except western areas.
Eggs: One to three. White.

Not easily seen, for its leaf-like plumage merges with the
trees in which it shelters during the day. Comes out at dusk
looking for insects near the ground, making a whirring
chirrupy sound. Nests in a hole in a tree.

EAGLE OWL (SPOTTED) *Bubo africanus*

L.: 43-47 cm. Colour: Mottled grey, blackish and white.
Features: Long tufts on head. Flight feathers and tail
broadly barred. Distribution: Throughout Southern Africa.
Eggs: Two to three. White.

A large formidable-looking owl, it usually sleeps during the
day. May be seen hunched up in a tree, or telegraph
pole. About dusk it awakens with a mournful hoot before it
flies off to hunt, usually in pairs. Builds a nest in bush-clad
ravines in rocky parts of a mountain.

NIGHTJAR (SOUTH AFRICAN) *Caprimulgus pectoralis*

L.: 23-25 cm. Colour: Dark dusky grey above, streaked with
black. Tawny wings. Features: White on side of face, and
throat. White spots on wing and tail tips.
Distribution: Southern Africa except dry areas.
Eggs: Two. Buff.

Not easy to spot during the day, for it may be lying flat on
a bough or squatting on the ground, looking like part of the
background with its leaf-like plumage. At dusk it may be
seen flying with leisurely wing-beats with its gape wide open
catching insects on the wing. Has a pleasant whistling call.
Lays its eggs on the bare ground.

SCOPS OWL

EAGLE OWL

NIGHTJAR

LITTLE SWIFT *Apus affinis*

Length 14cm. Colour: Sooty-brown. White rump.
Features: Square tail, pointed wings.
Distribution: Throughout Southern Africa. Not frequent in the south-western areas.
Eggs: One to three. White.

This neat little bird can be seen in large numbers, in towns and villages, sailing and twittering around their colony of clusters of nests under eaves of buildings. Sometimes seen away from civilization, where they build on overhanging cliffs or in caves.

COLY (WHITE-BACKED) *Colius colius*

L.: 30-34 cm. Colour: Grey and white back. Buffish below.
Features: Crest. Long stiff tail.
Distribution: Throughout Southern Africa except north-east.
Eggs: Three. Chalky-white.

Seen in large parties especially where there are fruit trees. It has a pet name of Mousebird, derived from the way of creeping in trees, its long tail and grey colouring looking very mouse-like. At dusk several can be seen bunched together holding on to a thin branch with their feet, in an upright position. A nest is a platform of twigs.

NARINA TROGON *Apaloderma narina*

L.: 29-34 cm.. Colour: Back, throat and chest, green. Wings black and grey. Red below. Features: Long tail broadly tipped with white. Heavy yellow bill.
Distribution: Mainly in forest areas in eastern parts.
Eggs: Three to four. White.

This resplendent bird inhabits the more tropical forest. It can be spotted making a short twisting flight, although its soft melancholy cooing can be heard before seeing it. It perches motionless for hours on a bough. Can sometimes be seen creeping about the branches in search for insects. Nests in a hole in a tree.

27

LITTLE SWIFT

WHITE-BACKED COLY

NARINA TROGON

PIED KINGFISHER *Ceryle rudis*

Length: 28 cm. Colour: Black and white all over.
Features: Long bill and crest.
Distribution: Throughout the waterways of Southern Africa.
Eggs: Four to six. White.

Often seen hovering over water—a black and white movement of rapidly-beating wings—before it plummets down on to a fish. Can also be seen perched on a rock or post for hours on end. It makes a tunnel in a bank which ends in a compartment for its nest.

MALACHITE KINGFISHER *Corythornis cristata*

Length 14cm. Colour: Dazzling blue above and orange below.
Features: Long pointed red bill and crest on head.
Distribution: Southern Africa except for arid areas.
Eggs: Three to five. Shiny white.

One of our smallest kingfishers, found where there is water or swampy ground. Seen like a brilliant flash as it skims over the water, or perched on a twig over the river before darting upon a fish. Has a way of lifting and lowering its blue crest. Makes a tunnel in the bank for a nest.

EUROPEAN BEE-EATER *Merops apiaster*

L.: 25-29 cm. Colour: Forehead white, predominantly blue and green, wings chestnut. Features: Two long tail feathers. Long, pointed, slightly down-curved bill.
Distribution: Throughout Southern Africa.
Eggs: Five to six. Glossy white.

A distinctive migrant, although a few breed in Cape Province and farther north. It is easily recognized by its brilliant plumage. Looks rather like a large swallow in flight soaring on its pointed wings and showing its pointed tail. Often spotted hawking insects on the wing, especially bees and locusts.

PIED KINGFISHER

MALACHITE KINGFISHER

EUROPEAN BEE-EATER

EUROPEAN ROLLER *Coracias garrulus*

L.: 30-31 cm. Colour: Exotic blue-green plumage. Chestnut back. Brilliant turquoise wings.
Features: Rolling flight. Strong hooked bill.
Distribution: Southern Africa except dry areas.
Eggs: Does not breed here.

This stoutly-built visitor from the north can be seen in scattered parties, in wooded areas during the summer months. A noisy bird, often spotted perched low on a tree or bush ready to swoop on to its prey.

GROUND HORNBILL *Bucorvus leadbeateri*

Length: 90 cm. Colour: Black body, red-ringed eyes, red throat and white-tipped wings.
Features: Long curving bill, long neck, short legs.
Distribution: Throughout Southern Africa, but mainly along East Coast up to Port Elizabeth.
Eggs: Two. Rough white.

This ungainly bird is seen in small parties, waddling and foraging and looking rather like a big black turkey. Can also be located by the loud booming noise it makes when feeding. Nests in a hollow in a tree or among boulders.

PIED BARBET *Tricholaema leucomelas*

L.: 17-18 cm. Colour: Red on crown and forehead. Black back and chest. White lower part. Yellow on head and base.
Features: Striped face. Short heavy curved bill.
Distribution: Throughout Southern Africa.
Eggs: Three to four. White.

This stout, distinctive little bird is commonly seen in pairs climbing trees in search of berries or fruit on which it feeds. A very noticeable ringing call. Bores a hole in a tree for a nest.

EUROPEAN ROLLER

GROUND HORNBILL

PIED BARBET

GROUND WOODPECKER *Geocolaptes olivaceus*

L.: 25-29 cm.. Colour: Head soft grey. Wings brown. White chest. Rose rump and belly. Features: Barred tail. Large pointed bill. Distribution: Confined to South Africa. Eggs: Three to five. White.

This purely indigenous species lives entirely on the ground. Is often seen on the mountain slopes moving about with awkward hops searching for insects and larvae on the rocks. For a nest it burrows a long hole into a bank with a nesting chamber at the end.

CARDINAL WOODPECKER *Dendropicos fuscescens*

L.: 14-16 cm. Colour: Crown to nape bright red. Mantle and wings blackish and green. Rufous on upper tail.
Features: Streaks on light breast, pointed brown bill.
Distribution: Throughout Southern Africa.
Eggs: Two to three. White.

A common bird in woodlands and forests. Usually seen in pairs. The male is very evident with red on back of head. May be seen climbing a tree or hanging on the bark and making rapid tappings. Nests in a stump of a tree.

LONG-BILLED LARK *Certhilauda curvirostris*

Length: 20 cm. Colour: Brown back, light underneath.
Features: Fairly long, curved bill and light eye stripe. longish tail.
Distribution: Throughout Southern Africa but more common in western areas.
Eggs: Two to three. Varying white to pink, with light spots.

A slim bird, but quite big for a lark. Usually seen in pairs. It flies up and, with a whistling call, comes gliding down again. Makes a nest of grass under a stone or tuft.

GROUND WOODPECKER

CARDINAL WOODPECKER

LONG-BILLED LARK

SPARROW LARK (CHESTNUT-BACKED) *Eremopterix leucotis*

Length: 13 cm. Colour: Black head and foreparts, chestnut wings and back. Features: White spot under eye and white on sides and rump. White ring round neck.
Distribution: Widespread throughout Southern Africa and mainly seen where there is open, stony ground.
Eggs: Two. Dirty white with brown freckles.

Is similar to the Grey-Backed Lark and both are distinguished by the white spot on the cheek. Although looking very sparrow-like, it does not hop but is seen walking or running. Makes a neat nest of dry grass on the ground.

EUROPEAN SWALLOW *Hirundo rustica*

Length: 18 cm. Colour: Steely-blue upperparts and whitish below. Glowing chestnut throat and brow.
Features: Swift flight and forked tail.
Distribution: Throughout Southern Africa.
Eggs: Does not breed here.

A common summer visitor, often seen by the hundreds perched on telegraph wires. A slender bird with a noticeably forked tail. Very often spotted skimming low over a pond, or sweeping to and fro in the upper air catching insects on the wing.

SAND MARTIN *Riparia paludicola*

Length 13 cm. Colour: Brown back, white underneath.
Features: Slightly forked tail, tiny bill.
Distribution: Throughout coast and country where there is permanent water.
Eggs: Two to four. White.

This little bird is usually seen skimming over the water in large numbers catching insects on the wing. For a nest it excavates a hole about two feet long either in a sandbank or in a sandy cliff. They nest close together.

SPARROW LARK

EUROPEAN SWALLOW

SAND MARTIN

BANDED MARTIN *Riparia cincta*

Length 17 cm. Colour: Mouse brown above. White below.
Features: Brown band across chest. White spot over eye.
Square tail.
Distribution: Throughout Southern Africa.
Eggs: Three to four: glossy white.

This little brown bird is often seen in pairs settling on
grass stems to pick off insects, or flying alone with deliberate
wing-beats. Usually near water or sandy places, where it
makes a long tunnel in a bank ending in a chamber for a nest.

DRONGO (FORK-TAILED) *Dicrurus adsimilis*

Length 25 cm. Colour: Black.
Features: Forked tail.
Distribution: Throughout Southern Africa.
Eggs: Two to four. White or cream, spotted with variations
of brown.

A conspicuous glossy bird, often spotted perched on telegraph
wires, hawking insects. Noisy when roosting in the trees. Is
bold and fearless. Builds a shallow saucer-like nest.

PIED CROW *Corvus albus*

L.: 46-52 cm. Colour: Black and white.
Features: Broad collar of white round neck, chest, and upper
belly.
Distribution: Most of Southern Africa.
Eggs: Three to six. Bluish-green, streaked and speckled with
olive-brown.

A conspicuous common crow. Pairs often seen by the roadside either scavenging for food or flying over with a harsh
guttural croak. Places a nest of sticks high in a tree.

BANDED MARTIN

DRONGO

PIED CROW

CAPE ROOK (BLACK CROW) *Corvus capensis*

L.: 48-53 cm.. Colour: Black.

Features: Sharp bill. Open wingtips in flight.

Distribution: Throughout Southern Africa.

Eggs: Three to five. Pinkish with mauve blotches.

These birds are usually seen in pairs on cultivated land, feeding mainly on insects and grain. It has a high-pitched, throaty chuckle. Makes a neat nest on the topmost branches of a high tree.

RAVEN (WHITE-NECKED) *Corvultur albicollis*

L.: 50-54 cm.. Colour: Black and white.

Features: Heavy bill, white half-collar.

Distribution: Mainly southern and eastern areas.

Eggs: Three to five, very pale blue, streaked with brown and olive.

A bold formidable bird often seen in pairs in mountainous parts. Not popular with farmers for it plunders poultry runs. Makes a nest of sticks, usually on a ledge.

PENDULINE TIT *Anothoscopus minutus*

L.: 9-10 cm. Colour: Darkish grey above. Light yellow below. Features: Black forehead. White under chin.

Distribution: Throughout Southern Africa, except northern and western parts. Eggs: Three to six. White.

Is the tiniest bird in Southern Africa, found where there is dry grass and thicket. Active and lively, easy to locate by its continual twittering whilst searching for food. Its nest, slung between twigs or branches, is a little closely-woven bag made out of wool or vegetable down. There is a false entrance, and the little bird closes the real one on leaving and returning to the nest to feed the young.

CAPE ROOK

RAVEN

PENDULINE TIT

BULBUL (RED-EYED) *Pycnonotus nigricans*

L.: 19-21 cm. Colour: Black head and neck. General sooty-brown effect with white front and yellow vent.
Features: Red round the eye, slight crest.
Distribution: Chiefly in the dry central and north-western areas.
Eggs: Three to five. Pale pink splattered with grey-brown.

A sociable, familiar bird in the garden, can be heard singing pleasantly. Has a habit of robbing trees of its fruit. There are one or two other similar species of this family with the same habits. Hides a bowl-like nest in a fork of a shrub or small tree.

SOMBRE BULBUL *Andropadus importunus*

L.: 19-23 cm. Colour: Above, olive green. Paler below.
Features: Sweet, clear, ringing song. Very pale eye.
Distribution: Scattered over Southern Africa.
Eggs: Two. Glossy white.

A common bird of the forest. Shy, often heard before seen hopping about the branches in search of berries or insects. Builds a shallow nest, usually placed in a fork of a tree.

THRUSH (OLIVE or CAPE) *Turdus olivaceus*

Length: 24 cm. Colour: Dark olive-grey above. Chin and throat white, streaked with dark brown. Remainder a tawny colour.
Features: Bright eye, yellow bill and legs.
Distribution: Mainly in the southern areas, but scattered over Southern Africa.
Eggs: Two to three. Greenish-blue, marked with rust.

Often seen plunging its bill into the lawn or grass for worms. Partakes of any cultivated fruit. When startled, it wings off with an alarmed whistle. Has a sweet clear song. Makes a cup-shaped nest in a shrub or small tree.

BULBUL

SOMBRE BULBUL

THRUSH

SENTINEL THRUSH *Monticola explorator*

Length: 18 cm. Colour: Head and neck blue. Back brown. Breast, deep orange. Features: Way of standing erect. Distribution. Mainly in the south.

Eggs: Three or four. Pale blue thinly spotted with rust colour.

An active and conspicuous bird, often spotted bolt upright on a rock standing sentinel from a commanding position. Sometimes prances about. Sings a cheerful, lively song. Builds a rough cup for a nest under a boulder or in a crevice.

CHAT (MOUNTAIN) *Oenanthe monticola*

L.: 17-20 cm. Colour: Black and white.

Features: Grey top of head. Black underneath. White edged tail. Distribution: Throughout Southern Africa.

Eggs: Two or three. Greenish-blue speckled with rufous.

A conspicuous bird of the mountain and hillside. Can be spotted soaring a little then suddenly dropping into a low rapid flight over the ground. Has a way of opening and shutting its wings and jerking its tail when perched. Has a very beautiful song. Makes shallow cup-like nest in a hole or under a rock.

CAPPED WHEATEAR *Oenanthe pileata*

Length 18 cm. Colour: Brown wings, black head, chest and tail, white eye-stripe, forehead, chin and rump.

Features: Flicks wings and jerks tail.

Distribution: Throughout Southern Africa.

Eggs: Three to five. Bluish-white, sometimes with reddish-brown spots.

Seen on the open bare ground, hopping about with wings flicking and tail jerking up and down as it looks for insects. Nests in a hole or under an antheap.

SENTINEL THRUSH

CHAT

CAPPED WHEATEAR

STONE CHAT *Saxicola torquata*

Length 14cm. Colour: Black, white and rufous.
Features: Black head, white flashes on wings, neck and tail base.
Distribution: Scattered all over Southern Africa.
Eggs: Three to four pale green, finely freckled with brown at thick end.

A plump, pretty little bird, often seen by the roadside usually in pairs, perched on a twig ready to fly down to pick up an insect from the grass or ground. Conceals nest in a tuft of grass.

ROBIN (CAPE) *Cossypha caffra*

Length 18cm. Colour: Dark head with white eye-stripe, rufous under tail and on breast and throat. Bluish-grey below.
Features: Beautiful song. Jerking tail.
Distribution: Throughout Southern Africa. Mainly south-west and southern.
Eggs: Three to four. Greenish-white, densly speckled with brown.

This perky, friendly little bird, is found in most gardens. Quite tame and often seen to flutter down near the house, and stand bobbing its tail up and down showing rufous underneath, or perched singing a clear warbling song. Makes a compact nest hidden well in a thick bush.

SCRUB ROBIN (WHITE-BROWED) *Erythropygia leucophrys*

Length 15cm. Colour: Mouse brown above, pale breast, black head, white eyebrow.
Features: Flashes of white on wings. Black streaks on chest.
Distribution: Mainly in the east.
Eggs: Two or three. Pale green freckled with rufous brown.

A shy little bird, often its flute-like whistling can be heard in the thicket. Like other robins it has a way of spreading its tail with jerks. Conceals its nest well in grass tuft or bush.

STONE CHAT

ROBIN

SCRUB ROBIN

WILLOW WARBLER *Phylloscopus trochilus*

Length 12cm. Colour: Olive green above. Pale yellow below.
Features: Pale yellow eye-stripe.
Distribution: Throughout Southern Africa except Cape.
Eggs: Does not breed here.

A migrant from Europe, and most abundant. Can be spotted flitting about in the foliage, making an occasional dash out to take an insect on the wing. Has a very sweet warbling song.

REED WARBLER (AFRICAN MARSH WARBLER)
Acrocephalus baeticatus

L.: 12-13 cm. Colour: Brown above. Buff below.
Features: Light throat. Pretty song.
Distribution: Throughout Southern Africa.
Eggs: Two to three. Pale greenish white, blotched with olive and grey.

This little brown bird is a common species from the large family of warblers. Seen near water and is quite tame. Builds a cup-like nest suspended in thick grass or reeds.

FANTAIL WARBLER *Schoenicola brevirostris*

L.: 15-16cm.. Colour: Russet brown above, darker tail. Paler below. Features: White-tipped fan-like tail.
Distribution: Throughout Southern Africa, over grassland areas, especially in eastern parts.
Eggs: Two. Creamy with lilac undermarkings mottled with reddish brown.

This little brown bird is often seen sitting on a grass stem emitting a loud whistle. Has a conspicuous jerky flight. Builds a frail cup-like nest in a tuft of grass.

WILLOW WARBLER

REED WARBLER

FANTAIL WARBLER

CROMBEC *Sylvietta rufescens*

L.: 10-12 cm. Colour: Greyish brown above, buff below. Features: Extremely short tail, longish slim-curved bill. Distribution: Throughout Southern Africa but mainly in dry thornveld. Eggs: Two. White, marked with variable brown or reddish spots.

This drab little warbler twitters ceaselessly and flips up and down as it chases for insects. Builds a neat little nest, bag-shaped and suspended from a twig.

DUSKY FLYCATCHER *Muscicapa adusta*

L.: 12-13 cm. Colour: Mouse brown above. White below. Features: White breast with dark streaks. Light eye-stripe. Distribution: Cape eastward through the coastal regions to Natal through to East Africa. Eggs: Three to four. Greenish, finely speckled with brown.

This little mouse-brown bird is fairly abundant in the wooded country. Can be spotted darting about after flying insects in the shade of the leaves. Sometimes seen perching on a low branch flicking its wings. Makes a neat cup-like nest bound with cobwebs, very well concealed in a bush.

TIT BABBLER (CAPE) *Parisoma subcaeruleum*

L.: 14-16 cm. Colour: Grey above. White throat. Grey and rufous below. Features: Black streaks under chin. Black tail with white ends. Distribution: Widespread, more common in south. Eggs: Two to three. White with blue-grey undermarkings and dark and pale sepia spots.

Excitable, cheerful, this little bird is found in open bushy country, singly or in pairs. Has a lovely trilling song. Makes a neat cup-like nest.

CROMBEC

DUSKY FLYCATCHER

TIT BABBLER

FLYCATCHER (PARADISE) *Terpsiphone viridis*

L.: 23-41 cm. Colour Chestnut back and tail. Malachite green-blue head. Pale grey vent.
Features: Two long tail feathers.
Distribution: Mainly in the south.
Eggs: Two to three. Pale cream with sparingly-sprinkled brownish spots.

An inquisitive, friendly little bird. It has a dainty graceful flight, with the two long tail feathers flowing behind. Its shining, crested head and rufous body makes it conspicuous in trees or bushes. Has a pretty, rippling warble. Makes a neat cup-like nest in a low fork of tree or bush.

WAGTAIL (CAPE) *Motacilla capensis*

Length 18cm. Colour: Above greeny-grey. Below yellowish-white. Black band round chest.
Features: Long wagging tail edged with white.
Distribution: Throughout Southern Africa.
Eggs: Three to four. Cream finely speckled with brown.

A friendly little bird seen in numbers, flying low or running swiftly over lawns to catch insects. Sometimes spotted at the coast running beside a wave. Builds a deep cup-like nest in holes, buildings or sometimes in creeper on houses.

YELLOW WAGTAIL (BLUE-HEADED) *Motacilla flava*

Length 18cm. Colour: Olive-brown above. Yellow underparts.
Features: Longish tail which dips up and down ceaselessly.
Distribution: Near water. Mainly eastern areas.
Eggs: Does not breed here.

A gay little migrant from the north. Often spotted running or dancing up after insects on lawns or following the plough. Can sometimes be seen in large numbers around rivers and lakes. Has a brief warbling song.

FLYCATCHER

WAGTAIL

YELLOW WAGTAIL

PIPIT (PLAIN-BACKED) *Anthus leucophrys*

Length 18 cm. Colour: Brown above. Pale buff below.
Features: Brown flecks on breast, buff eye-stripe.
Distribution: Throughout Southern Africa, where there are grassy plains.
Eggs: Three. White, speckled with light brown spots.

This slim brown bird can be seen in a flock. Has a habit of moving its tail up and down whilst running on the ground. Conceals nest under a tuft of grass.

FISCAL SHRIKE *Lanis collaris*

Length 23 cm. Colour: Black and white.
Features: Sharply-hooked bill. Conspicuous white V on back.
Distribution: Throughout Southern Africa.
Eggs: Three to five. Greenish, spotted with pale brown, and blotches of purplish brown.

A bold distinctive bird, often called Butcher Bird, because of its predatory habits of making a larder by impaling its prey on thorns. Very often seen in pairs or alone perched on a branch or telegraph pole. Shows a lot of white on edge of tail when it flies off. Makes a compact nest in fork of tree.

RED-BACKED SHRIKE *Lanius collurio*

Length 18 cm. Colour: Back and wings chestnut. Grey head and rump. Pale pinkish buff below. Features: Broad black and white tail, white throat, black eye-stripe.
Distribution: Throughout Southern Africa.
Eggs: Does not breed here.

A migrant from Europe, may be seen all the year round, but mostly in the summer. It is usually spotted on a perch with a commanding view, quietly watching, before darting down on to an insect. Makes a harsh call note.

PIPIT

FISCAL SHRIKE

RED-BACKED SHRIKE

CRIMSON-BREASTED SHRIKE *Laniarius atro-coccineus*

Length 23cm. Colour: Crimson below, black top and wings with white bands.

Features: Unmistakable by its colour. Sharp, turned-down bill.

Distribution: Mainly found in Kalahari and South-Western areas and scattered throughout Southern Africa.

Eggs: Two to four. Pale-green, spotted and blotched with brown and grey.

This beautiful bird is usually found where there is matted thornbush. It can be heard making a loud, deep, whistling note from the depths of the bush. Makes a shallow, cup-like nest.

PUFFBACK SHRIKE *Dryoscopus cubla*

Length 18cm. Colour: Black and white.

Features: White, long, hairy feathers on rump, sometimes puffed up.

Distribution: Southern Africa, where there are trees.

Eggs: Three. Cream sprinkled with sepia spots.

Often seen in small parties in forest, open woodland and bushes. Its name arises from the habit the male has of puffing up the white patch of feathers on its back and rump when it is excited, making it look like a snowball. Makes a cup-like nest bound with cobwebs, found usually in the fork of a tree, fairly high from the ground.

LONG-TAILED SHRIKE *Urolestes melanoleucus*

Length: 40-50 cm.

Colour: Black with white back and wing flashes.

Features: Long white-tipped tail and has a magpie look.

Distribution: Throughout thornveld of Southern Africa. Not commonly seen in southern areas.

Eggs: Four to five. Pinkish-buff with speckles and spots.

Usually seen in small parties. Has dipping flight. Sometimes seen hunched up on a branch or telegraph wire. Has a loud whistling call. Nests are a strong bowl shape and made in a thornbush.

CRIMSON-BREASTED SHRIKE

PUFFBACK SHRIKE

LONG-TAILED SHRIKE

BOKMAKIERIE *Telophorus zeylonus*

Length: 23cm. Colour: Yellow underparts. Heavy black collar. Olive-green above. Features: Distinctive duet call. Dark tail with yellow edges in flight.
Distribution: Widespread throughout Southern Africa.
Eggs: Three. Greenish-blue marked with rusty brown.

This handsome tame bird of the shrike family is often seen perched very erect, singing a duet with its mate. Pairs can frequently be spotted dashing on to the grass for insects. Makes a big compact nest in thicket.

EUROPEAN STARLING *Sturnus vulgaris*

Length 20cm. Colour: Metallic iridescent blue-black flecked with white. Features: Yellow pointed bill.
Distribution: Mainly in Cape but spreading.
Eggs: Three to five. Pale blue.

A pest to fruit-growers, this species was introduced from Europe. It has an aggressive manner and way of walking. Makes a whistling sound. Nests in buildings and trees.

RED-WINGED STARLING *Onychognathus morio*

Length: 27cm. Colour: Blue-black. Red wing tips.
Features: Distinctive red on wings.
Distribution: Mainly southern and eastern areas.
Eggs: Three to five. Bluish-green with a few red-brown spots and blotches.

This shining blue-black bird loves a garden with fruit. Can be heard making a rather melancholy, loud melodious whistle from the roof-top. Commonly seen in large parties, or roosting in the rocks up the mountain where it nests.

BOKMAKIERIE

EUROPEAN STARLING

RED-WINGED STARLING

SUGARBIRD (LONG-TAILED) *Promerops cafer*

L.: 37-44 cm.. Colour: Brown above. Buff below.

Features: Yellow under tail. Long curved bill, extremel
long tail. Distribution: Southern Cape Province from
Oliphants River to Grahamstown.

Eggs: Two. Buff with streaks and blotches of brown.

This decorative bird is peculiar to South Africa. Whereve
there are Protea bushes, you are likely to see this distinctiv
bird. It has a habit of dancing in the air over a bush, with i
long tail flowing in the breeze. Makes a bowl-shaped nes
well concealed in a bush.

PIED STARLING *Spreo bicolor*

L.: 25-27 cm.. Colour: Dusky brown and white.

Features: Easily recognized by white vent.

Distribution: South Africa only.

Eggs: Three to five. Greenish-blue.

This bird is seen in the open veld where there are tree
and likes to roost in a flock. Often seen flying singly i
search of food—soft fruit and insects—and sometime
feeding among cattle. Nests under the eaves of a farmhous
or building.

MALACHITE SUNBIRD *Nectarinia famosa*

L.: 23-25 cm. Colour: Metallic green.

Features: Wedge tail with two long feathers, long curve
bill. Yellow under wing in flight.

Distribution: Southern Africa, except north-western area

Eggs: Two. Cream, finely speckled with greyish-brown.

This elegant sunbird is generously distributed on the lowe
slopes of mountain and hillside, where there are flowerin
shrubs. Its metallic-green glints as it is seen flitting restlessl
from bush to bush, showing the yellow tufts under its wing
Makes a pear-shaped nest suspended from a branch or bush

SUGARBIRD

PIED STARLING

MALACHITE SUNBIRD

SUNBIRD (ORANGE-BREASTED) *Anthobaphes violacea*

L.: 13-17 cm. Colour: Head and throat metallic-green. Violet band on chest of orange. Underparts yellow. Tail an wings greenish-black. Features: Dark wedge-shaped tai Slender, curved bill. Distribution: Confined to the mountair of the southern and eastern Cape Province. Eggs: One to two White, covered with streaks and dots of greyish-brown.

Tame and conspicuous, this little bird can often be see flitting about the Erica bushes on the open hillside an mountain, making a cheerful squeaking sound. Builds dome-shaped nest usually in a bush.

SUNBIRD (LESSER DOUBLE-COLLARED) *Cinnyris chalybeus*

L.: 12-13 cm. . Colour: Malachite green head, neck an upper wings. Tail blackish. Narrow metallic blue band, an red on breast. Features: Long curved, slender bill.
Distribution: Throughout Southern Africa except for wes Eggs: Two. Mottled grey.

This common little sunbird is found where flowers ar plentiful. Not at all shy. Its long bill enables it to extrac nectar from tubular-like flowers. Seen and heard in partie: Suspends nest from branch in a bush or small tree.

BLACK SUNBIRD (AMETHYST) *Chalcomritra amethystina*

Length 15 cm. Colour: Deep purplish black. Metalic gree head. Features: Violet patches on tail, throat, and shoulder: Long curved slender bill.
Distribution: Mainly southern and eastern Cape Province Eggs: Two. Creamy with suffused blotches and streaks.

This rich velvety looking bird is widely distributed wher there are aloes and plenty of flowers from which it takes th nectar with its slender curved bill. Sometimes seen in partie flying rapidly. Makes a pear-shaped nest suspended from high twig in a bush.

ORANGE-BREASTED
SUNBIRD

LESSER DOUBLE-COLLARED
SUNBIRD

BLACK SUNBIRD

WHITE EYE (GREEN) *Zosterops virens*

Length 13 cm. Colour: Moss-green and yellow.
Features: White ring round eye.
Distribution: Southern Cape Province. Some eastern areas.
Eggs: Two to three. Pale blue.

This tame little bird can be seen in small parties, busy and
restless, among the bushes and foliage. Constantly twittering
whilst searching for insects. Builds a deep, finely-woven cup
for a nest.

YELLOW-THROATED SPARROW *Petronia superciliaris*

L.: 15-16 cm. Colour: Above, dusky earth-brown. Below
greyish-white. Features: Broad buff stripe over eye. Small
yellow spot on neck.
Distribution: Southern Africa except western Cape.
Eggs: Three. Shiny buff heavily mottled with dark brown.

This cheerful little brown bird is common in woodland areas
where there is water. Often seen walking in a sprightly
manner looking for insects and seeds, making a loud
chirruping all the time. Nests in holes in trees.

SPARROW (CAPE MOSSIE) *Passer melanurus*

L.: 14-16 cm. Colour: Black head with white round eye.
Chestnut on back. White below.
Features: White eye-stripe.
Distribution: South West Africa and southern parts.
Eggs: Three to six. White or greenish.
The most distinguished of the sparrow family. This friendly
little bird is plentiful in towns and villages. Often seen
hopping vigorously about in the garden, looking for insects.
Builds an untidy nest under eaves, or in creeper on the wall.

WHITE EYE

YELLOW-THROATED SPARROW

CAPE SPARROW

MASKED WEAVER *Ploceus velatus*

Length 15cm. Colour: Rich yellow underneath, brown wings. Black face and forehead.

Features: Black mask. Chatters incessantly.

Distribution: Throughout Southern Africa.

Eggs: Two to three. Green closely spotted with brown.

Found in colonies by waterways and reedbeds. The male is particularly conspicuous in his breeding dress. He can be seen busy building kidney-shaped nests suspended from the end of a branch or reeds, while his less-colourful mates line them inside.

RED-BILLED QUELEA *Quelea quelea*

Length: 13cm. Colour: Light brown above, white with pink breast below. Features: Red bill and black face.

Distribution: Throughout Southern Africa but less common in extreme west and south.

Eggs: Three to five. Pale blue, sometimes freckled.

Breeds in large numbers over most of Southern Africa. Most gregarious and a pest. Swarming flocks will destroy a field of grain in a short time. The male is colourful but in winter he is a little brown bird like his mate. Nests are woven into trees or bushes.

RED BISHOP *Euplectes orix*

Length: 14cm. Colour: Crimson with black head and chest.

Features: Very brilliant colouring. Bouncy flight.

Distribution: Throughout Southern Africa.

Eggs: Three. Turquoise.

The male is a polygamous bird and most pugnacious during the breeding season when the bright colours are most evident. The female is always drab. In some places the equally-dazzling yellow species is seen in the company of the red. They make a clapping noise with their wings. An oval nest attached to a reed is built.

MASKED WEAVER

RED-BILLED QUELEA

RED BISHOP

WAXBILL (COMMON) *Estrilda astrild*

Length: 13 cm. Colour: Greyish-brown above. Pinkish underparts.
Features: Crimson on face and belly, with fine wavy lines.
Distribution: Widespread throughout Southern Africa.
Eggs: Four to five. White.

This small bird is found commonly where there is water. Very tame, and usually seen in flocks feeding on the ground. Is a popular cage bird. Makes an untidy nest near the ground in grassy tuft or bank. The nest has a projecting entrance.

PINTAIL WHYDAH *Vidua macroura*

L.: 26-34 cm.. Colour: Mantle tail and wings black. White underpart and on rump. Dark brown wings with white.
Features: Very long tail.
Distribution: Mainly over Southern Africa.
Eggs: Number not recorded. Cream.

Conspicuous near cultivated grassland. The male with its long tail is often accompanied by several drab-coloured females with short tails. Has a restless flight, and a way of dancing in the air with a jerking tail. Parasitic on waxbills' nests.

CANARY (CAPE) *Serinus canicollis*

Length: 13 cm. Colour: Golden-green above. Yellow below.
Features: Trilling song.
Distribution: Southern and eastern parts.
Eggs: Three to four. Greenish white speckled with brown.

Very common in the wooded areas. Frequently seen in large flocks, trilling on top of trees. Parties often seen flying to the ground to feed on seeds of grass. Often kept in captivity for its sweet song. Builds a cup-shaped nest low in a bush.

WAXBILL

PINTAIL WHYDAH

CAPE CANARY

CAPE SISKIN *Serinus totta*

Length: 13cm. Colour: Dark brown back, olive and yellow underparts.
Features: White tips to wings and tail. Pale eye-stripe.
Distribution: Southern Africa where there are mountains.
Eggs: Three to five. Pale greenish-blue. Sparsely speckled at thick end mostly with dark brown.

This pretty, lively little bird, attracts attention when seen in small flocks on the mountainside. Inhabits the scrub where it sings a pleasant little song. Makes a cup-like nest in a low shrub or crevice.

LARK-LIKE BUNTING *Fringillaria impetuani*

L.: 13-14 cm. Colour: Dark brown wings, upperparts dusky-brown, chin and throat pale buff.
Features: Lively song. Pale-buff eye-stripe.
Distribution: Common throughout Southern Africa and most abundant in Karoo and Namaqualand.
Eggs: Two to four. Pale-green, finely speckled.

This pretty little bird can be seen flying off in large parties or feeding on the ground or near a waterhole. Makes a neat, shallow cup-like nest.

BUNTING (CAPE) *Fringillaria capensis*

Length: 13cm. Colour: Earth brown.
Features: Striped face.
Distribution: Throughout Southern Africa. Common in Western Cape. Occurs in hills and mountain.
Eggs: Two or three. White with thick markings of pinky-brown and mottled grey.

This little brown bird is widely distributed, but with colour and markings varying slightly. It can always be recognized by its striped face, and grey underparts. Has a pleasant little song on the wing. Makes a bowl-shaped nest in a bush or tuft of grass.

CAPE SISKIN

LARK-LIKE BUNTING

BUNTING

INDEX

Numbers in italics denote Roberts' nomenclature.

FIELD NOTES

FIELD NOTES

FIELD NOTES

FIELD NOTES

FIELD NOTES

FIELD NOTES

FIELD NOTES

FIELD NOTES

FIELD NOTES

FIELD NOTES